DEADLY DISASTERS

THE CORONAVIRUS PANDEMIC

BY NATHAN SOMMER

BELLWETHER MEDIA · MINNEAPOLIS, MN

Torque brims with excitement
perfect for thrill-seekers of all kinds.
Discover daring survival skills, explore
uncharted worlds, and marvel at mighty
engines and extreme sports. In *Torque* books,
anything can happen. Are you ready?

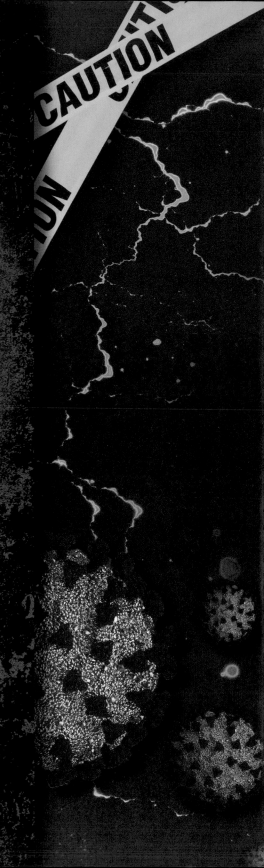

This edition first published in 2022 by Bellwether Media, Inc.

Library of Congress Cataloging-in-Publication Data

Names: Sommer, Nathan, author.
Title: The coronavirus pandemic / by Nathan Sommer.
Description: Minneapolis, MN : Bellwether Media, 2022. | Series: Deadly
    disasters | Includes bibliographical references and index. | Audience:
    Ages 7-12 | Audience: Grades 4-6 | Summary: "Amazing photography
    accompanies engaging information about the coronavirus pandemic. The
    combination of high-interest subject matter and light text is intended
    for students in grades 3 through 7"–Provided by publisher"– Provided
    by publisher.
Identifiers: LCCN 2021021972 (print) | LCCN 2021021973 (ebook) | ISBN
    9781644875261 (library binding) | ISBN 9781648344343 (ebook)
Subjects: LCSH: COVID-19 (Disease)–Juvenile literature. | Communicable
    diseases–Juvenile literature.
Classification: LCC RA644.C67 S63 2022 (print) | LCC RA644.C67 (ebook) |
    DDC 614.5/92414–dc23
LC record available at https://lccn.loc.gov/2021021972
LC ebook record available at https://lccn.loc.gov/2021021973

Editor: Kieran Downs   Designer: Josh Brink

Printed in the United States of America, North Mankato, MN.

TABLE OF CONTENTS

CAUTION

AGAINST THE ODDS

Geoffrey McKillop was about to become a grandfather. But he was having trouble breathing. He had coronavirus. Soon, he needed to go to the hospital.

Geoffrey was placed on a **ventilator**. He spent two weeks fighting for his life. But he survived! On April 25, he left the hospital. He soon met his newborn grandson!

BAD CASE
Only the worst coronavirus cases need ventilators.

GEOFFREY MCKILLOP

oxygen

HOW PANDEMICS BEGIN

Pandemics happen when **infectious** diseases spread quickly around the world. Most happen because of new illnesses. People are not **immune** to them yet.

The coronavirus pandemic began with a **virus**. It spread through **droplets**. People who breathed in infected droplets got coronavirus. The disease spread more quickly in crowded places.

HOW CORONAVIRUS SPREADS

SMALL DROPLETS

- spread through talking
- travel farther
- may float in the air for longer

LARGE DROPLETS

- spread through coughing and sneezing
- do not travel far

CORONAVIRUS SYMPTOMS

Early coronavirus warning signs include a runny nose and a sore throat. Loss of taste or smell is also common.

The coronavirus pandemic was caused by the COVID-19 virus. It first spread in Wuhan, China, in late 2019. Many scientists believe the virus started in bats. Bats spread it to other animals. Then, it spread to humans.

The virus spread to nearby countries in early 2020. The **WHO** announced a global pandemic on March 11, 2020.

WUHAN, CHINA

BEHIND THE NAME

The CO in COVID-19 stands for corona. The VI stands for virus. The D stands for disease. The 19 represents the year that the virus was discovered.

WHO ANNOUNCING
THE PANDEMIC

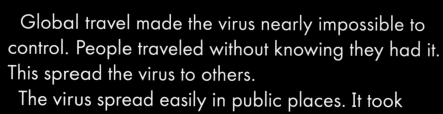

Global travel made the virus nearly impossible to control. People traveled without knowing they had it. This spread the virus to others.

The virus spread easily in public places. It took months to teach people how to stop its spread. Even then, many did not act safely.

AREAS AFFECTED

AT LEAST ONE COVID-19 CASE =

JANUARY 23, 2020

MARCH 1, 2020

MAY 22, 2020

DAMAGE AND DESTRUCTION

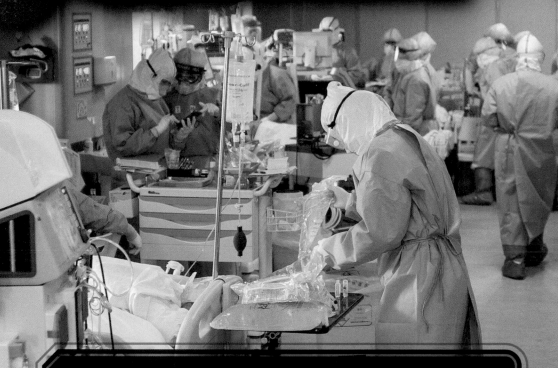

The virus had infected more than 154 million people by May 2021. Millions of them needed to be treated in hospitals. Many did not live.

Many hospitals ran out of beds. Others ran low on ventilators. Doctors and nurses became sick at work. This meant hospitals did not have enough workers.

NEW DAILY COVID-19 CASES IN THE UNITED STATES

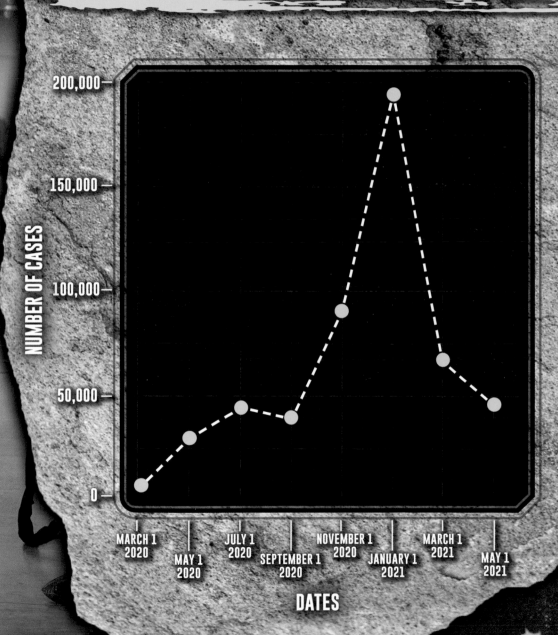

NUMBER OF CASES

200,000

150,000

100,000

50,000

0

MARCH 1
2020

MAY 1
2020

JULY 1
2020

SEPTEMBER 1
2020

NOVEMBER 1
2020

JANUARY 1
2021

MARCH 1
2021

MAY 1
2021

DATES

More than 100,000 U.S. companies went out of business during the pandemic. Many people lost their jobs. More than 8 million Americans fell into **poverty**. Black and Hispanic people struggled the most.

Many people could not afford food or housing costs. There were also **shortages** of many products. The pandemic cost the U.S. **economy** an estimated $16 trillion.

TIMELINE

NOVEMBER 17, 2019
The first known case of COVID-19 is contracted

MARCH 11, 2020
The WHO declares the coronavirus outbreak a global pandemic

NOVEMBER 8, 2020
The number of COVID-19 cases worldwide passes 50 million

JANUARY 1, 2021

The United States passes
20 million COVID-19 cases

DECEMBER 14, 2020

Health care workers in the
United States begin receiving
the coronavirus vaccine

APRIL 19, 2021

All U.S. adults are allowed to
get the COVID-19 vaccine

THE WORLD FIGHTS CORONAVIRUS

Governments passed new laws to fight the virus. Many ordered people to wear masks in public. Others created **lockdowns**. Many governments tried to help people without jobs. Most adults in the U.S. got money.

Stores limited the number of people that could shop at one time. Large events were canceled. People worked and studied from home.

LONG-TERM HEALTH EFFECTS

Most people with COVID-19 recovered in a few weeks. But the virus increased the risk for long-term heart and lung problems in many patients.

Life without pasta is not.

#Pappardelle

WHOLE FOODS MARKET

Please respect social distancing guidelines by waiting behind the taped lines.

Thank you.

Scientists around the world started working on a **vaccine** right away. The first vaccine was approved in December 2020.

In the U.S., health care workers and people in nursing homes were vaccinated first. Other **frontline workers** and older people came next. By April 2021, all adults were allowed to get the vaccine.

COVID-19 VACCINE

COVID-19
Pfizer
Vaccine 1 ml
2020-2021
Injection Only

Batch
2020-201

only for
medical
use

19

CORONAVIRUS SAFETY

SOCIAL DISTANCING

Social distancing became a new rule during the pandemic. Most people kept far apart in public spaces. They also wore masks. Experts used the pandemic to study how viruses spread. They also studied how the disease affected people. There is still a lot to learn about the coronavirus pandemic!

PREPARATION KIT

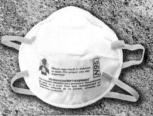

MASKS

THERMOMETER

CLEANING SUPPLIES

HAND SANITIZER

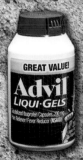

FEVER REDUCERS

GLOSSARY

droplets—very small drops of a liquid

economy—money created from the goods and services an area produces

frontline workers—those who continue to work with the public during a pandemic

immune—protected against something

infectious—easily spread to others

lockdowns—laws passed by governments to stop the spread of coronavirus; lockdowns closed many schools and limited customers in businesses.

poverty—the state in which people do not have enough money to pay for food, clothes, or shelter

shortages—events during which there is not enough of something needed

social distancing—keeping a safe distance between yourself and people you do not live with

vaccine—a powerful medicine that helps increase protection against harmful diseases

ventilator—a machine that helps people breathe when they cannot breathe on their own

virus—something that takes over cells in people's bodies to make them sick; a virus can be easily spread from person to person.

WHO—World Health Organization; the World Health Organization is the global agency responsible for controlling worldwide public health.

CAUTION

CAUTION

AT THE LIBRARY

Goldstein, Margaret J. *Heroes of the Pandemic*. Minneapolis, Minn.: Lerner Publications, 2022.

Hopkinson, Deborah. *The Deadliest Diseases Then and Now*. New York, N.Y.: Scholastic Press, 2021.

Hudak, Heather C. *What is a Virus?* New York, N.Y.: AV2, 2020.

ON THE WEB

FACTSURFER

Factsurfer.com gives you a safe, fun way to find more information.

1. Go to www.factsurfer.com

2. Enter "coronavirus pandemic" into the search box and click 🔍.

3. Select your book cover to see a list of related content.

INDEX

The images in this book are reproduced through the courtesy of: Limbitech, cover (hero), CIP; Manoej Paateel, cover (frontline workers); faboi, cover (medical tent); Liam McBurney/ Alamy Stock Photo, pp. 4-5; Godlikeart, pp. 6-7; Robert W/ Alamy Stock Photo, pp. 8-9; Xinhua/ Alamy Stock Photo, pp. 9 (WHO), 12-13; Real_life_Studio, pp. 10-11; Batchelder/ Alamy Stock Photo, pp. 14-15; Jennifer M. Mason, pp. 16-17; Tada Images, p. 17 (sign); Steven May/ Alamy Stock Photo, pp. 18-19; Carlos I Vives, p. 19 (vaccine); Trekkathon, pp. 20-21; Olexandr Panchenko, p. 21 (mask); frantic00, p. 21 (thermometer); Yuganov Konstantin, p. 21 (cleaning supplies); tab62, p. 21 (hand sanitizer); Ken Wolter, p. 21 (Advil); Chansak Joe, p. 21 (Tylenol).

CAUTION   CAU